WEATHER

Scientists

Debra J. Housel, M.S.Ed.

Earth and Space Science Readers:
Weather Scientists

Publishing Credits

Editorial Director
Dona Herweck Rice

Associate Editor
Joshua BishopRoby

Editor-in-Chief
Sharon Coan, M.S.Ed.

Creative Director
Lee Aucoin

Illustration Manager
Timothy J. Bradley

Publisher
Rachelle Cracchiolo, M.S.Ed.

Science Contributor
Sally Ride Science

Science Consultants
Nancy McKeown
Planetary Geologist
William B. Rice
Engineering Geologist

Teacher Created Materials
5301 Oceanus Drive
Huntington Beach, CA 92649-1030
http://www.tcmpub.com
ISBN 978-0-7439-0552-7

Printed in China
Nordica.032020.CA22000192

Table of Contents

Early Weather Scientists

Long ago, weather was a mystery. People thought the gods made the weather. The ancient Greeks believed the god Zeus sent lightning bolts to the earth when he got angry. People believed the myths because they had no other way to understand weather. No one knew how to measure heat, cold, or wind.

In 1564, Galileo Galilei was born in Italy. He was interested in many things. He could paint and play music, but he also loved science. He solved the mystery of how to measure heat and cold. He did this by making the first **thermometer**. His work and his life led others to study science, too.

Later, Galileo's student made the first **barometer**. A barometer measures **air pressure**. High pressure often means dry, sunny weather. Low pressure often means wet weather and storms.

Observing the Sky

Galileo made many discoveries. He was especially skilled in **astronomy**. Astronomy is the science that studies outer space. Galileo's work helped us to understand how the sun, moon, and planets move.

Gabriel Daniel Fahrenheit

Years passed. Not much progress was made in the study of weather. Then, Gabriel Daniel Fahrenheit was born in 1686. His parents both died when he was young. He had to work hard as a shopkeeper to make enough money to live. However, his real passion was science.

Fahrenheit knew that earlier thermometers were flawed. The **temperature** changed with air pressure on Galileo's thermometer. Other designs had problems, too. Fahrenheit found a way to make the thermometer more accurate. He decided to use **mercury**. Mercury swells with heat. It shrinks as it gets colder. It rises and falls at a steady rate.

Mercury forms into droplets like these at room temperature.

At 212°F freshwater boils.

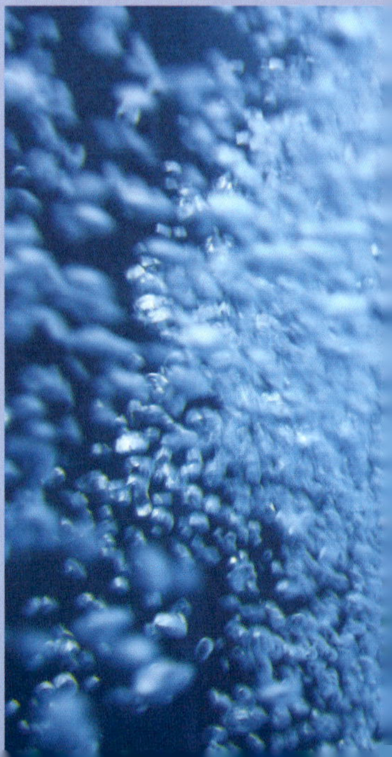

It works over a wide range of temperatures. Best of all, in a thermometer, mercury gives exact measurements!

Fahrenheit marked two points on his new thermometer. The temperature where saltwater froze was marked at 0°F. His body temperature was marked at 100°F. Between those two, freshwater froze at 32°F. It boiled way up at 212°F. At last, people could record and compare temperatures accurately.

At 32°F freshwater freezes into solid ice.

Today's Weather Scientists

Today, there are many ways for people to get weather reports. Often, they watch **meteorologists** give reports on television. But meteorologists don't just report the weather. They need to know how to study and predict it before it occurs. That way, we can prepare for different types of weather. We can take precautions if a storm is brewing. We can plan a weekend trip to the beach if sunny days are ahead. Mish Michaels is an important television meteorologist. Her career is filled with awards for her work in weather.

The **Fahrenheit temperature scale** is used today only in the United States. Most nations and scientists everywhere use a different scale. It is called the **Celsius temperature scale**. Many people invented it at about the same time. It is named after Anders Celsius, an astronomer and one of the scale's first developers.

Celsius was born in Sweden. He was interested in astronomy. There weren't many learning opportunities in his country. His desire to learn led him on a grand tour of Europe. He visited many famous astronomy sites. When he came home, he built Sweden's first **observatory**. That is a place used to watch and study space.

Celsius was one of many people who used the **centigrade scale**. Centigrade uses the freezing and boiling points of freshwater to mark the ends of a scale. It split the range between those points into 100 equal degrees. Freshwater boils at 100°C. It freezes at 0°C. (Celsius had it the other way around at first.) Temperatures below zero have a minus sign. In 1948, the scale's name was changed to honor Celsius for his efforts.

Thermometers compare Fahrenheit and Celsius scales.

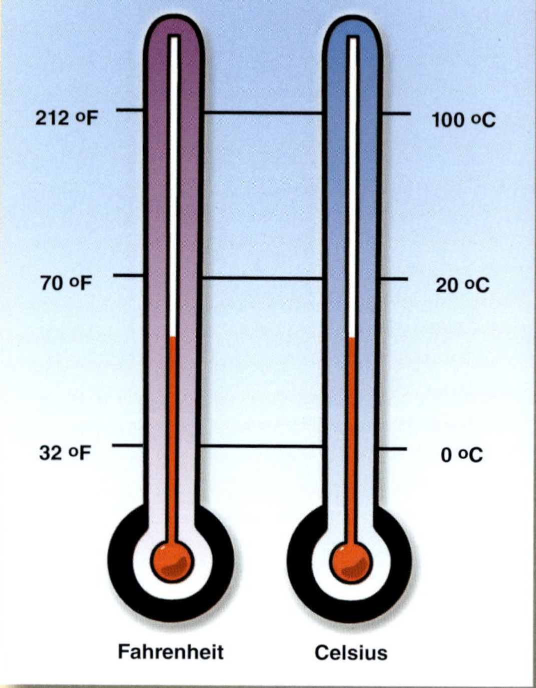

Extreme Temperatures

The highest temperature ever recorded on Earth was 57.8°C (136°F) in North Africa. The coldest temperature ever was -89.2°C (–128.6°F) in Antarctica.

Gaspard-Gustave de Coriolis was born in France in 1792. He was a very good student and worked hard to get a good education. When his father died, he had to support his family. First, he became a math tutor. Finally, he was offered a job as a professor of mechanics. During this time, he did research. Then, he made an important discovery. Today, it is known as the **Coriolis force**.

Coriolis noticed that things moving over rotating bodies, like the earth, did not move in a straight line. Coriolis noticed that air moving north or south from the equator did not move in a straight line. North of the equator, air curves to the right or east. South of the equator air curves to the left or west. The Coriolis force affects the direction of winds. It helps explain the movement of hurricanes.

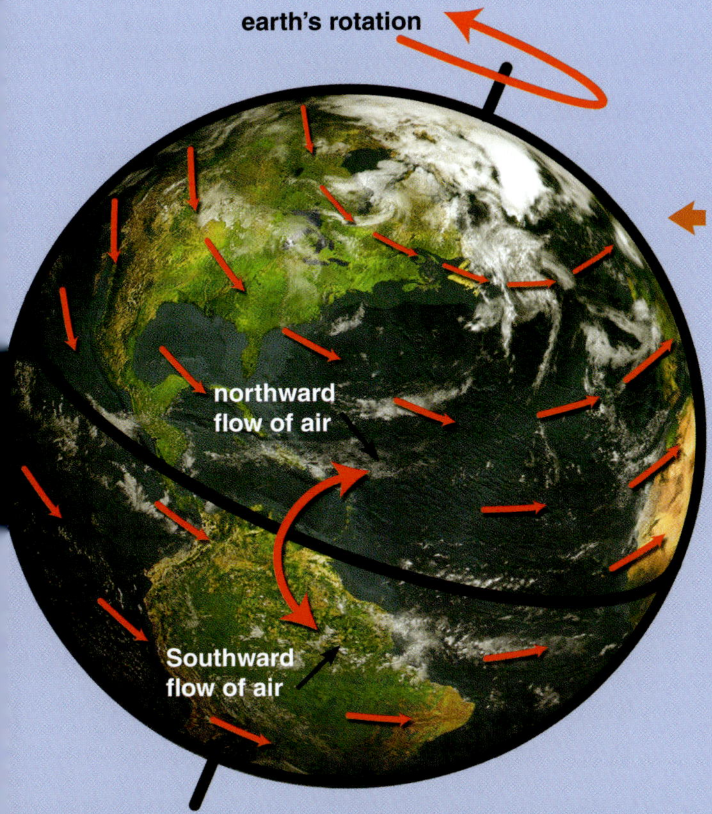

diagram of the Coriolis force

This satellite image shows the wind patterns that move clouds across the face of the earth.

Susan Solomon

When Susan Solomon was in high school, she won third prize in a national science fair. Her project measured the oxygen found in gas mixtures. It's not surprising that she grew up to be an atmospheric chemist. That means that she studies the chemistry of atmospheres. Some of her most important work in this field has been the study of the hole in the ozone layer of Earth's atmosphere.

Coriolis Force

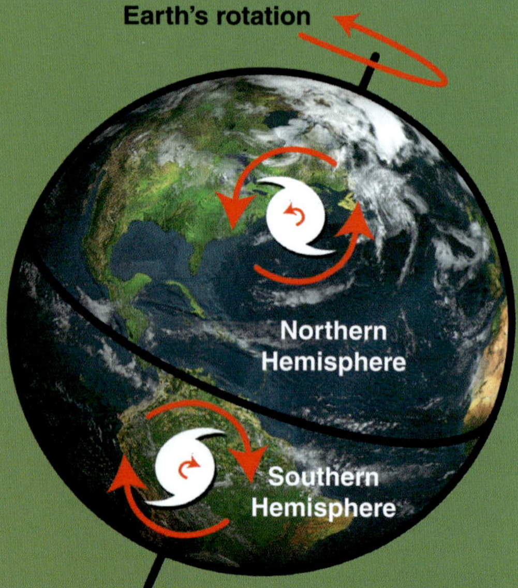

Cyclones, like tornadoes and hurricanes, rotate counterclockwise in the Northern Hemisphere. In the Southern Hemisphere, cyclones rotate clockwise.

A good example of the Coriolis force is the eye of a hurricane. In the Northern Hemisphere, the wind to the north of a hurricane blows west. The wind to the south of a hurricane blows east. This makes the wind swirl around the hurricane's eye in the center. In the Southern Hemisphere, everything is reversed, so the hurricane spins in the opposite direction.

At the equator, the Coriolis force is zero. Hurricanes can't form there. Most form at least 500 kilometers (310 miles) north or south of the equator. Why? Well, the further from the equator, the stronger the Coriolis force.

The First!

Whatever the great accomplishment, there is always a first! June Bacon-Bercey is the first woman and first African American to be awarded top honors from the American Meteorological Society. The group gave her its "seal of approval" for excellence in television weathercasting.

Meteorologists use many tools to forecast the weather.

Forecasting the Weather

People first tried to guess the weather in 650 B.C. They used cloud patterns. They could only predict the next day, and they were usually wrong.

Modern forecasting began with the telegraph in 1837. It let people know what weather was coming toward them. Now, many tools gather data. **Weather satellites**, radar, and weather balloons send the data to computers. The computers come up with a forecast. We see them on the news or on the Internet.

Computers are not perfect, though. Some experts believe that a human can make a better prediction for the next six hours of weather than a computer can!

Weather satellites can project images of hurricanes like this one off the coast of Florida.

Benjamin Franklin

In America, Benjamin Franklin is best known for his work in founding the United States. He was a great politician. Franklin accomplished many other things in his life, too. He was a great weather scientist.

Franklin studied the **Gulf Stream**. The Gulf Stream is a warm water current that runs through the Atlantic Ocean. Franklin charted its course. He kept records of its temperature, speed, and depth. He found that it moves north along the east coast of the United States. Then it turns and crosses the sea. The wind blows across it and keeps Europe warm.

The Gulf Stream, as mapped in Franklin's time

Storm Chaser

To really understand storms and how they work, you've got to get into them. That's part of the work done by Robbie Hood. Hood studies the atmosphere. She hunts hurricanes! Hood works with a team on an airplane that actually flies into hurricanes. The airplane has special sensors that collect information about the atmosphere. Hood's studies will help scientists predict when hurricanes are forming.

Robbie Hood

A research airplane approaches the eye of a hurricane.

Benjamin Franklin was also interested in electricity. He suspected that **lightning** was electricity. In 1752, he thought of a way to prove it. He wrote a paper about flying a kite during a thunderstorm with a metal key attached to the kite. It is commonly believed today that Franklin did fly such a kite in a storm. But there is no proof that he did anything more than have the idea. However, other people did try his idea.

Lightning did not strike the kite. However, the kite and string did become charged. When it happened, the loose threads of the string stood upright. In this experiment, Franklin not only proved that lightning is bolts of electricity but also that storm clouds are charged.

Franklin knew that lightning was very dangerous. So, he invented the **lightning rod**. It grounded a lightning bolt by moving the charge from the rod into the ground. This keeps a home or barn from catching fire. When lightning struck Franklin's home, its worth was proven. His home was not harmed.

Dr. Lightning

Ben Franklin could have used someone like Mary Ann Cooper nearby during his experiments. She is a doctor who researches injuries caused by lightning. Such injuries can be serious and even deadly. The work of Dr. Cooper and others like her may save many lives over time.

Lightning Strike!

An Australian park ranger has been struck by lightning seven times. He is still alive! Twice his hair caught fire. Another time he lost a toenail and his eyebrows.

There are two kinds of lightning. The most common is negative lightning. One of its bolts has enough energy to light a 100-watt bulb for two months. Positive lightning is more dangerous. It has enough energy to light a 100-watt bulb for 95 years!

The safest place to be during a lightning storm is indoors. If you are outside, do not stand under a tree. Lightning may hit it. If you are in an open field, lay down and make yourself as flat as possible.

Continuing the Work of the Weather Pioneers

Sir Robert Alexander Watson-Watt was born in Scotland in 1892. After college, he researched how to use radio signals in order to find lightning. In the late 1930s, he developed **radar**. Radar uses radio waves to locate things. During World War II, his studies led to the construction of radar stations in England. These stations guided ships and found enemy planes.

Radar is useful in other ways, too. It can be used to detect rain and snow. This led people to think of using radar to study weather. In 1942, the U.S. Navy gave the Weather Bureau 25 radar stations. This started the world's first weather radar system. It gave data on snow, rain, and cloud cover.

Radical Radar

Today, radar has become so advanced that we can use it to "see" one bee up to 29 kilometers (18 miles) away!

Sir Robert Alexander Watson-Watt

In 1955, the old Navy radar was changed to use the Doppler effect. **Doppler radar** is one of the most important weather developments ever. Its name comes from Christian Doppler. In 1842, he observed that motion affects the pitch of sound waves. Doppler radar uses this effect to see not only where things are, but how fast they are moving.

Christian Doppler

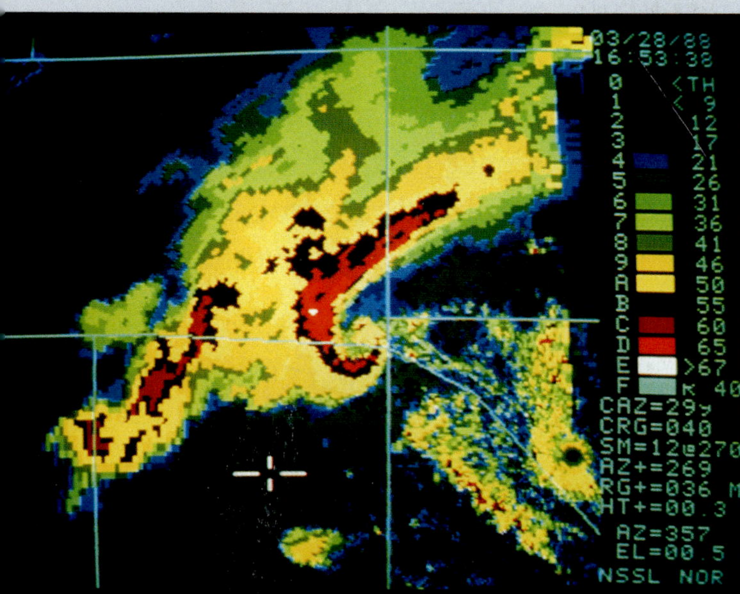

a sample Doppler image showing the typical "hook" of a developing tornado

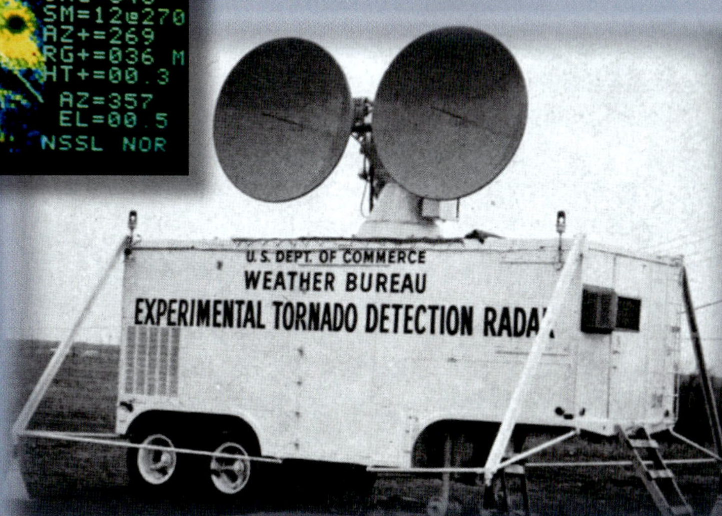

first experimental Doppler radar unit

All's Clear

When a space shuttle is launched, safety demands that the weather conditions be right. Scientists like Katherine Winters of NASA have an important job to do. Winters is a shuttle launch weather officer. She gives weather reports before, during, and after a launch. Without her work, a launch could not happen.

How does that work? Well, think about the sound of a train's whistle. Its pitch seems higher as it comes toward you and lower as it moves away. Really, the pitch remains the same. But as the train gets closer to you, more sound waves reach your ear in a given amount of time. You hear the pitch rise. As the train moves away from you, the opposite happens. You hear the pitch fall.

What does this have to do with weather? Doppler radar was applied to weather science because it can detect the speed of wind and raindrops. It can tell the difference between the tone it sends

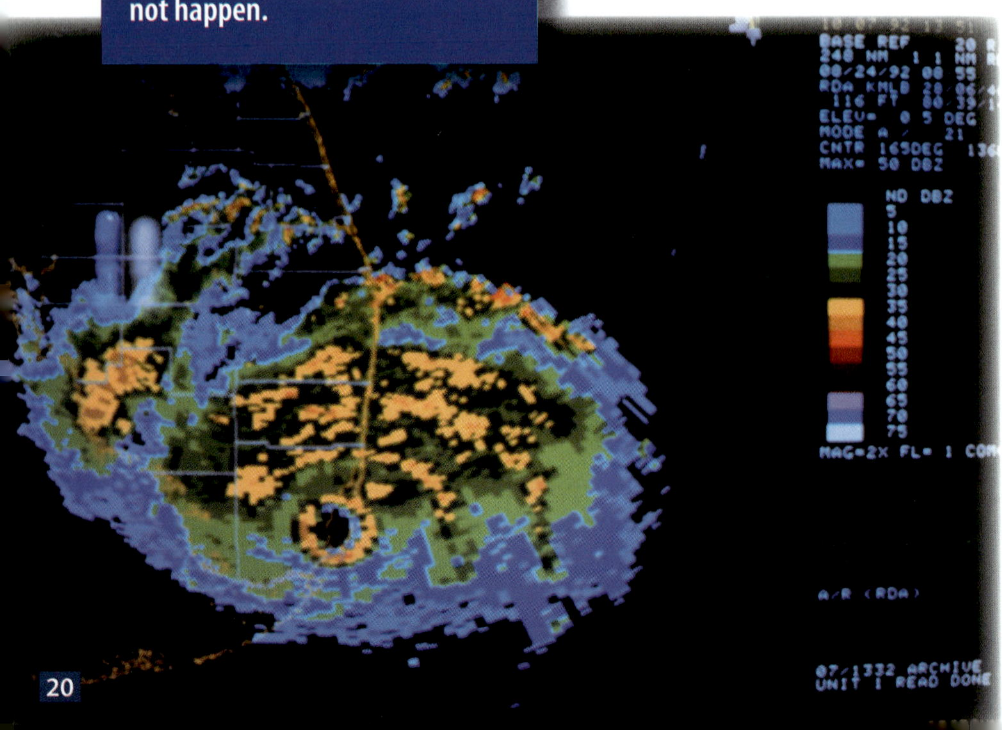

This is a Doppler radar image of a hurricane. The colors relate to rainfall, with blue and black showing light rain and orange and red showing heavy rain.

out and the one it gets back. It also knows which way the raindrops are moving. It even changes all this data into pictures. People have learned how to read these pictures to make predictions. This is yet another technique that scientists use to forecast the weather.

Today's Technology

Courtney Schumacher is a radar meteorologist. She was part of the team that sent the first radar into space in 1997. This special radar is used to measure weather. Schumacher studies precipitation systems. By using radar, she can collect lots of information over time. This data will help explain why rain falls when it does. That way, we can better forecast future storms. This is just one of the many ways that scientists use new technology to study weather. What technology do you think the future might bring?

Schumacher working in her lab

During the past century, many scientists made advances in the study of weather. One scientist worth noting is Tetsuya Theodore Fujita. He was born in Japan in 1920. In school, he studied engineering. As an adult, he moved to the United States to continue his research.

Tetsuya Theodore Fujita

Fujita studied hurricanes and tornadoes. He was the first to realize that several twisters can spin off from a single funnel cloud. In 1967, he made the first color movie of Earth. He used pictures taken from a satellite. The pictures showed cloud motion. This technique is now used in weather reports on television.

Later, with the help of his wife, Sumiko, Fujita made the Fujita Scale. The scale rates tornadoes based on their wind speeds and their ability to cause destruction. This scale earned him the nickname "Mr. Tornado." Fujita showed how studying data can improve our knowledge of weather. Never before has so much data been available.

Charles Keeling

Protecting the Planet

There are many amazing weather scientists who work to protect our planet. They study things that affect Earth's atmosphere. Scientist Charles Keeling is a good example. He did many studies on **climate**, which is the average weather in an area over a period of time. Keeling was also the first scientist to confirm the accumulation of carbon dioxide in our atmosphere. Too much carbon dioxide in the atmosphere may warm up the whole planet. This can be harmful to our environment. Keeling's studies help us know what problems exist in our atmosphere.

The first weather satellite went into space in 1959. Now many satellites circle Earth. They take images that can help predict a storm's path. Today, some scientists race toward twisters. They set up radar to get data from inside the funnel. Pilots fly into storms to take measurements. More than 50,000 weather stations around the world share climate data. Having all of this information has led to major advances in our understanding of weather.

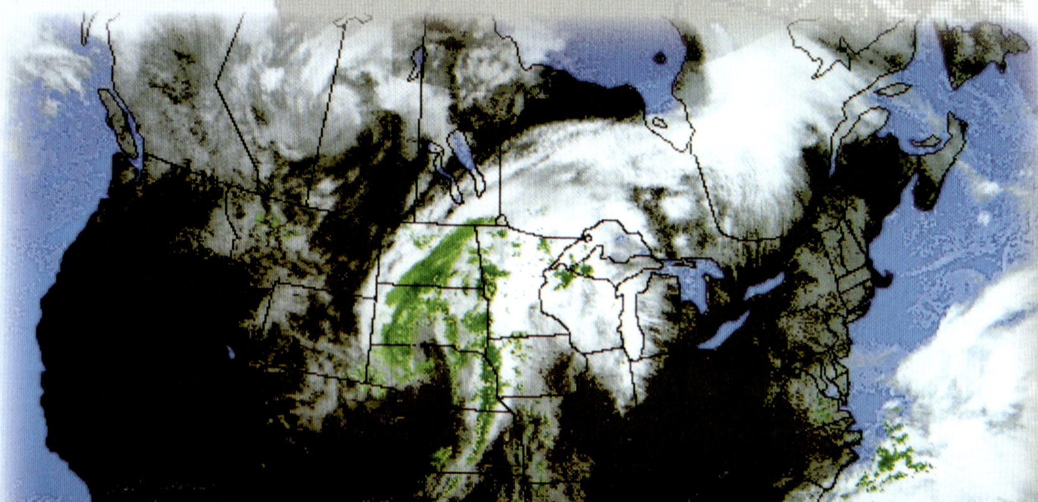

This satellite image of Hurricane Francis was taken over Florida on September 5, 2004.

We are still at the mercy of storms. But with better predictions, fewer lives are lost. We get warnings of blizzards, hurricanes, and tornadoes. We have a good idea of when and where they will strike, so we can get out of their way. For that, we can thank the weather scientists.

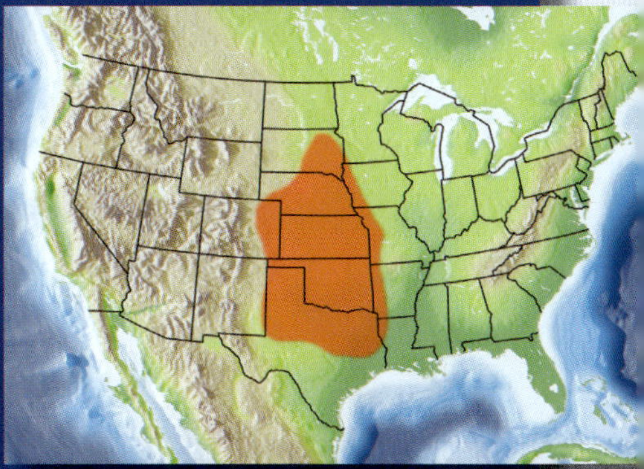

Tornado Alley

Three out of every four tornadoes occur in the United States. Because so many tornadoes roar through Oklahoma, northern Texas, and other central states, this area has earned the nickname "Tornado Alley."

Treacherous Typhoons

Typhoons are hurricanes that strike Asia. They are extremely powerful. They can cause massive destruction. In 2004, ten typhoons hit Japan. That was a record. Fortunately, advance forecasts helped to reduce the loss of life.

observation satellite orbiting Earth

Climate Scientist: *Inez Fung*

University of California, Berkeley

Sky Science

Believe it or not, when Inez Fung was a young girl in Hong Kong, she liked typhoons. "I loved the wind, rain, and waves. And when they hit, school was canceled."

Fung also loved math. Then, when she was in college, a professor told her about meteorology, the science of weather. It was perfect, because she could use math to explain typhoons.

Now, Fung studies Earth's climate. She focuses on a gas called carbon dioxide (CO_2). She has made some important discoveries about CO_2 by using powerful computers.

Fung's love of typhoons such as this one started when she was a young girl.

Fung completed high school in Hong Kong and then came to the United States for college.

Did you know that people can affect our climate? Things like pollution can cause the temperature to rise. That's called **global warming**. Fung wants to use her smarts to understand and prevent it. "I decided to apply mathematics to the future of climate, and the future of the planet."

Being There

If you were a climate scientist, you might . . .

- collect ice at the North Pole.
- investigate how pollution affects our climate.
- build satellites to study the atmosphere.

Think About It

Do you live on a farm? Near the ocean? In the desert? Weather plays an important role in your life. What are some ways that the weather has affected your family's life?

Experts Tell Us

Fung says, "You have to know math, physics, chemistry, and biology to see how the whole planet is connected."

Lab: *How Raindrops Form*

In this experiment, the bottom of the jar is Earth's surface. The warm water is water on the surface of the sea. The salt makes it like ocean water. The jar lid is high up in the atmosphere. The ice cubes simulate the temperature of the upper troposphere, the layer of atmosphere closest to Earth.

Materials

- $\frac{1}{4}$ cup hot water (not boiling)
- clean, dry clear glass jar with a screw-type metal lid (16 oz. salsa jar is ideal)
- $\frac{1}{4}$ t. iodized or kosher salt (not a reduced-sodium salt such as Salt Sense)
- 4 ice cubes
- cotton swab with two ends
- scissors

Procedure

1 Put salt into the bottom of a clean, dry glass jar.

2 Pour hot water into the jar. Stir the mixture with the measuring spoon.

3 Stick the cotton swab into the water. Taste it to be sure that it's salty.

4 Use scissors to snip off the used end of the cotton swab.

5 Place the lid upside down on top of the jar.

6 Put four ice cubes on top of the lid.

7 Observe the underside of the lid after 15 minutes. Record what you see.

8 Use the cotton swab to absorb one of the drops condensed on the underside of the lid. Taste it. Record if it tastes salty or fresh.

2

6

7

Conclusion

Water from the ocean evaporates into the atmosphere. It condenses when it rises high into the atmosphere due to the cold temperatures there. This condensation forms rain droplets. However, when water evaporates from the oceans, it leaves the salt behind. This explains why hurricanes form over salt water yet drop freshwater.

Glossary

air pressure—the force of air pushing against a surface such as your body or the earth

astronomy—the scientific study of the universe and of objects in space such as the moon, sun, planets, and stars

barometer—an instrument used to measure air pressure

Celsius temperature scale—a measurement of temperature using a scale on which freshwater boils at 100 degrees and freezes at 0 degrees; originally called the centigrade scale.

centigrade scale—the earlier name for the temperature scale used by Anders Celsius and other scientists before it was renamed

climate—the usual weather in a place

Coriolis force—a natural phenomenon that causes air to curve to the right north of the equator and to the left south of the equator

Doppler radar—equipment that uses an antenna and radio waves to detect wind and precipitation as well as the speed of light

Fahrenheit temperature scale—a measurement of temperature using a scale on which freshwater boils at 212 degrees and freezes at 32 degrees

global warming—an overall rise in local average temperature around the world

Gulf Stream—a warm water current starting in the Caribbean Sea and flowing across the Atlantic to Europe

lightning—a flash of high-voltage electricity that moves from one charged cloud to another or from a charged cloud to the ground

lightning rod—a metal wire fixed in a high place to conduct the electricity released from a lightning bolt into the ground

mercury—a silvery-white liquid metallic element commonly used in thermometers and barometers

meteorologist—a scientist who studies Earth's atmosphere, climates, and weather

observatory—a building or place designed for making astronomical observations

radar—a device used to find solid objects by reflecting radio waves off objects and receiving the reflected waves; originally an acronym for radio detecting and ranging

temperature—a degree of heat or cold

thermometer—an instrument that measures temperature

weather satellite—a spacecraft sent into orbit hundreds to thousands of miles above Earth that monitors and photographs conditions in the atmosphere

Index

Sally Ride Science

Sally Ride Science™ is an innovative content company dedicated to fueling young people's interests in science. Our publications and programs provide opportunities for students and teachers to explore the captivating world of science—from astrobiology to zoology. We bring science to life and show young people that science is creative, collaborative, fascinating, and fun.

Image Credits

Cover: Gene Blevins/LA Daily News/CORBIS; p.3 Photos.com; p.4 DiMaggio/Kalish/CORBIS; p.4–5 DiMaggio/Kalish/CORBIS; p.5 The Granger Collection, New York; p.6 (top) Bettmann/CORBIS; p.6 (bottom) Mediacolor's/Alamy; p.6 (right) Shutterstock; p.7 (left) Archana bhartia/Shutterstock; p.7 (right) courtesy CBS4 (WBZ-TV, Boston); p.8 (top) Mary Evans Picture Library/Alamy; p.8 (bottom) Tim Bradley; p.9 (top) AM Corporation/Alamy; p.9 (bottom) iStockphoto; p.10 (left) Rick Reason; p.10–11 NASA/Photo Researchers, Inc.; p.11 (top) Tim Bradley; p.12 (left) Tim Bradley; p.12 (bottom) Rick Reason; p.13 (top) Visuals Unlimited/Corbis; p.13 (bottom) Phil Degginger/Alamy; p.14 (top) The Granger Collection, New York; p.14 (bottom) Tim Bradley; p.15 Dennis Olive/NASA; p.15 (background) NOAA; p.16 Courtesy of Mary Ann Cooper; p.16–17 A & J Verkaik/CORBIS; p.18 (top) NSSL/NOAA; p.18 (bottom) Fox Photos/Getty Images; p.19 (left) NSSL/NOAA; p.19 (top) Hulton Archive/Getty Images; p.19 (bottom) NOAA; p.20 (top) NASA; p.20 (bottom) NWS/NOAA; p.21 Courtesy of Courtney Schumacher; p.22 Courtesy of University of Chicago; p.22–23 JIM REED/SPL/Photo Researchers, Inc.; p.23 Courtesy of Charles Keeling; p.24 Carolina K. Smith, M.D./Shutterstock; p.24–25 Carolina K. Smith, M.D./Shutterstock; p.25 (left) Cristi Matei/Shutterstock; p.25 (top) Tim Bradley; p.26 (top) Jim Bishop; p.27 Warren Faidley/Corbis; p.28 (top) Paul Maguire/Shutterstock; p.28–29 Nicoll Rager Fuller